AND ONE MORE THING

I Brake for Squirrels and Other Thoughts
I Have No Doubt About

Kay Thomas

KAY THOMAS

4/6

ISBN 978-1-300-16095-3

Author information at www.kathomaswriter.com

DEDICATION

For Mom, Dad and Dot no longer with me
For Christine and Ken
For Larry

D - p.47

CONTENTS

FOREWORD

"What is most personal is most universal," wrote the American psychologist Carl Rogers, whose work ushered in a new understanding of mental health as a human-centered process that takes into account the broad collection of experiences we all pick up in a life time. For some, writing down observations and memories is a kind of therapy that unlocks forgotten connections between past events and present opportunities. In the case of Kay Thomas' writings, it becomes therapy for the readers as well.

As a newspaper editor who is always on the lookout for talented columnists who can entertain and surprise my readers, I find Kay's work to be a treasure trove. Her writing isn't always local or topical, but it's always relevant — raising issues that people at every stage of their lives will encounter. Kay's voice is distinct and inviting. Reading an installment of "…And one more thing" is like sitting with her at the corner coffee shop while, with a twinkle in her eye, she holds court about matters dear to her.

As a parent of young children, I am especially delighted when Kay relates her observations of parents trying to wrangle their kids into some semblance of civil behavior in restaurants and other public places. She both sympathizes with our plight and lets us off the hook. I also enjoy her travelogues, which become less about the places she visits and more about the process of traveling itself. On my own trips, I try to emulate her sense of discovery and appreciation.

Kay helps you cope — with aging, changing technology and with how to simply slow down and notice the rich bounty our world provides.

Kay's best essays are collected here in one place, organized thematically so collectively, they lead you through a cohesive journey. If you've experienced Kay's newspaper columns week after week, you'll more clearly see in this book how the ideas of one lead to and influence another.

If you're new to the work of Kay Thomas, please let me introduce you to a new friend.

Mark Gillespie

Livingston County News

INTRODUCTION

It took a lifetime to get these thoughts down on paper. First, I had to live them with the help of family, friends and colleagues. "Life has been good," the saying goes, although like everyone else, I have had my challenges.

I have loved to write my entire life. At thirteen I pronounced myself a full-fledged journalist. I started the *Lincoln Street Gazette*, a neighborhood newspaper that I reported, edited, published and sold for two cents per copy. It continued sporadically all the way through my high school years. Those were the days of typewriters and carbon paper. Enough said.

Writing poetry and short stories kept my creative juices flowing during my thirty-year teaching career. Journals and boxes were stuffed with bits and starts of ideas that never got off the ground. Someday, I thought.

When I took stock of myself after retirement, I realized that I had something to say that hopefully could benefit others. Certainly, it would be a shame not to share my insights. In what form or manner I had no clue, until I was lucky enough to take on a challenge to write for the *Genesee Country Express,* Dansville, NY, through an invitation from the then editor, DJ Smith.

Fortunately, DJ was willing to impart his knowledge, while I stumbled along learning the art of the journalistic style. His patience with my raw abilities and natural passion was incredible. He showed me techniques to turn good writing into outstanding pieces, and he didn't let up on me one bit. And even better, it was DJ who first recognized that my best writing was my personal observations with all their quirky, detailed stories.

I developed a column, "…*AND ONE MORE THING*," social commentary on life's lessons from my standpoint, and brought it to the attention of Mark Gillespie, managing editor of the *Livingston County News,* Geneseo, NY. I was hired to write a bi-weekly column in February 2011, and it was a comfortable fit. The column has evolved, and my essays tackle current social issues in a broader sense as well.

This book is filled with columns that readers have told me were their favorites. There are a couple of pieces that hold special meaning in my heart. Several have not found their way into print. Take them for what they are worth, and enjoy.

Things Pull Me Every Which Way

I don't know where the saying originates, although on one level it has playful visual appeal. "Things pull me every which way" was one quirky phrase I heard on the lips of my mother growing up. She was known in our family circle for her use of clever statements, and probably would be considered an accomplished wordsmith by others outside the fold.

It is written in reference to properly training a puppy to walk beside his master on a leash, with the warning clearly spelled out done otherwise, there are consequences to pay. Picture the cheeky puppy managing the frustrated owner, and leaping and jumping—you guessed it, every which way.

A scientist says that electrons act like magnets pointing every which way, more or less equal numbers pulling or pushing. That's quite the energetic frolic like executing a passionate Latin salsa twirling a man and woman by opposite attraction back and forth over the dance floor.

A horse trainer remarked that if she didn't teach her horse the correct way to jump obstacles, the horse might go every which way shying away at the last moment before a crucial command.

I was a little kid with an unlimited capacity to pretend way beyond the ordinary without batting an eyelash. I could summon it up at a moment's notice keeping myself entertained during long hot summers. Fanciful dreaming came in handy when I waited at my grandparents' stuffy house—seen but not heard, while my mother took care of grown-up business often lasting endlessly in my opinion. I had more important things on my agenda like swimming and sitting on the beach with my friends.

One afternoon an occurrence of a spooky kind pulled me every which way. The oppressive air waved over me like a magician's wand and I thought that I was having trouble breathing. I felt closed in. My strength was zapped. The thick mauve drapes hindered the light and any outside noise. These were all the characteristics of a panic attack before the term became popular. Still all the monsters and space aliens were after me wherever I went. I couldn't get away.

When I tried to assume exactly what those words my mother peppered her conversations with seasoned to perfection —every which way, I would literally feel my body parts—my spindly arms and legs, being yanked and stretched in all different directions at the same instant jerking me oddly off balance. I had no control. My two braids stood on end like they were lathered in glue and my scalp stretched away from my head to arrive at a pointy tip. Circling in my brain were the most bizarre modernistic black and white scribblings of orbiting spaceships, fairies and voyagers in no particular order heading into a vast emptiness. I was thrown into the mix like a lost soul with no proper destination. Cool!

Somehow, I would take just so much of this fantasizing before I would hold on to myself two arms wrapped around my chest and slink back into the soft sofa to protect my very own body from escaping me. Mind you, I hadn't moved an inch, but I envisioned differently. Breathing a sigh of relief, I lifted up my eyes to check if anyone had noticed? Nope. Safe again. The adults were deep into a discussion of a clambake for the Fourth of July, firecrackers…hmmm… interesting stuff and worth leaning in for a bit.

After a period of those suffocating experiences, and I wasn't making any headway to Mars, the moon or wherever, I figured that enough was enough. I went back to reading biographies of Jane Addams and Thomas Jefferson pulling one after another off the racks at the public library. That was the summer I had given myself to the life-altering goal of reading the entire library's fiction collection in order. In between bios and novels, I left the sci-fi alone in their far corner out of sight. It was better to let someone else have the adventure and keep my feet on the ground.

I was abandoning ship—that every which way or that. I found out how others lived life. I was hoping for a clue or two about my own. Alas, later I did go back to sci-fi and fantasy, as the draw was too great. The world was becoming less understandable as I got older, and space travel was in vogue. My imagination always did get the best of me and I did get pulled every which way although I am not sure that it harmed my writing one bit.

Recently, with the passing of one of the greatest writers in America—Ray Bradbury, I find myself drawn to re-reading his book, "Zen in the Art of Writing," and low and behold, I am recollecting that his childhood was similar to mine in how we both thrived on its playfulness.

Bradbury and I were people watchers and relatives were our first resource. He put those characters into "The Martian Chronicles" and "Dandelion Wine" among other stories too numerous to mention. He must have chuckled to himself later about sitting through insignificant family gatherings that became the backbone of his stories. I am doing that myself, and dredging up more and more promising tidbits.

If I had to pick the turning point in my writing when it went from every which way to what it is today, I would have to say it was when I figured out how to let my inner voice take over and deal with all the experiences deep within me. The words started to flow without any control from me and my detailed take on life's truths became my best work. The muse no longer came in spurts, but ordered my ideas with hands off from me. Thank goodness.

As Ray Bradbury said, "relax, stop thinking and write."

You betcha'.

Match Your Clothes to Fit Your Courage

What you wear presents an image open to interpretation, and there is no way to get around it either.

Clothing is little more than a basic covering, although our modern cultural fascination with style and fashion goes way to the other extreme. Take for example, the focus on Kate Middleton's wedding dress, or media hype over a popular NBA player's body tattoos.

Attire speaks of an individual. You have among your friends and family members possibly one or two that you might be quick to say are outrageous dressers, but perhaps they are courageous, too, if you look at it differently.

Katherine Hepburn put on pants in the 1940s and made fashion history way a head of her time. She was her own person, and her clothing made a statement. You absolutely could classify her as rebellious and independent.

There were others, too, like Amelia Earhart. She went against the grain with more important things to accomplish in life, and she wore her courage on her sleeve.

Think how long it took businesses and schools to accept female employees wearing pants, and— perish the thought— going without stockings. The casual Friday dress code followed. Then women applauded the courage of a new generation of mothers-in-waiting showing off their baby bumps in the 90s when Demi Moore set the standard on Vanity Fair's 1991 cover.

Clothing can define an even broader commitment to society.

On 9/11 while workers from the Twin Towers were running away to safety, the brave New York City uniformed police and firemen were doing their jobs, and going in the more difficult direction. There were plenty of off duty officers that "internally" wore their uniforms into the burning buildings as well, following their professional oaths.

There is a well known saying going around the Internet that proclaims, "Every morning when a policeman or a fireman put on a uniform there is a complete act of selfless courage along with it. They do not know what they are going to face when they walk out the door."

The same goes for our military. They are sons, daughters, husbands, fathers, wives and mothers; whether or not you agree with the usefulness of war, these men and women are serving their country.

Now you might argue that clothing and acceptable dress has gone down the tubes. Clothing makes a statement whether it might be good or bad, intentional or not.

Can you ever forget Jerry Seinfeld is his pink puffy shirt and Cher in her get-ups? Take a look at reruns from early sitcoms, and there have been courageous dressers way before today.

"I wear clothes as I don't have the courage in this society not to," one freethinking feminist informed me in no uncertain terms.

A teacher went to school in a pair of green Capri slacks and a purple polo shirt. She thought that she looked a bit preppy, since her usual attire was much more "theatrical."

As she was beginning her first lesson the room erupted with giggling.

"OK, what's the joke?"

One brave soul responded, "You look like Barney."

She laughed and said, "That wasn't exactly the look I was trying to achieve, but I'm glad I've brought back a happy childhood memory."

Frantically trying to suppress his laughter another boy said, "What look were you trying to achieve?"

She said that she was putting together colors found in nature. From the back of the room came grumbling that green and purple are never found together in nature.

"You never see purple and green in the forest? What about tulips, lilacs and grapes?"

Grunts were made in acknowledgement. Courage can be there on both sides of the classroom when a teacher and her students can enjoy honest laughter together.

If you go to a festival you will encounter every imaginable statement on a t-shirt indicating someone's status. There are particular t-shirts that catch your eye because they courageously make a statement from "I support same sex marriage," to "save the planet from fracking."

The pink shirt symbolizing a breast Cancer survivor prompts you to pause a moment and think of the tough road someone walks. It forms solidarity between wearers as well. Their courage is difficult to put into words, but they journey forward together.

My 90-year-old gym friend used to get on the treadmill wearing the title of a poetry book on her sweatshirt saying, "When I Am an Old Woman I Shall Wear Purple." I asked her what it felt like to be her age.

"I feel the same as an 18 year old," was her quick comeback with a grin on her face. "I guess I am courageously living my life day to day."

For a colorblind individual facing the constant challenge with dressing, you hope that he has loving assistance.

Teaching a youngster how to match prints and stripes properly can be a slow go, but doable task. Maybe it's fashionable to experiment with lines and angles, anyhow, and throw that fashion rule out once and for all.

You might feel at top form wearing a classic outfit from thirty years ago that shows off the splendor of a different decade.

For those of you who's daily routine includes polishing your medals on a uniform, you should hold your head up high.

Consider that you put on a badge of courage when you dress each day. You are your unique self.

A Dilemma of the Littlest Kind

I brake for squirrels and other living creatures that might cross my path while driving. No duck or chipmunk needs to worry which side I am on in the war of pavement survival.

Now on the quiet back roads where I wander it is fine to do that without compromising safety too much. My environmentally conscious friends tell me that when I do brake, I destroy those tiny guys' sense of timing. It's all part of their day's work and those road vibrations are what they are tuned to catch. Hmmm… I never thought of that.

Yesterday I took particular notice of a squirrel that darted out in front of me and I instinctively slowed waiting to hear "The Thump," but alas, the little guy tiptoed backwards dancing his tango step to safety. I drove on relieved tapping my happy fingers on the steering wheel, while my young friend fled into the bushes.

Speaking of "The Thump," a friend told me that when she heard what I was writing about she was concerned that I didn't have the sound description right at all. According to her it is "Thump-pause, de thump." The thought of one "thump" is painful enough for me to think of.

Those pesky chipmunks scurry around playing havoc with car wiring, too. I found that out the hard way when my auto mechanic told me what was causing my engine light to come on resulting in costly repairs. Fortunately the warranty kicked in and saved me a bundle. Sometimes it doesn't win to try to live in harmony with those little critters. Mothballs in the car grille I am told will do the trick. They'll have to relocate to another garage.

"Make Way For Ducklings" is a classic children's picture book written and illustrated by Robert McCloskey. First published in 1941, the book tells the story of a pair of mallard ducks that decide to raise their family of eight ducklings on an island in the lagoon in the Boston Public Garden, a park in the center of the city.

The message is clear. Both children and adults learned to live peacefully with the duckling family respecting them as creatures of the earth thrust in the midst of towering buildings and the hustle and bustle of city life. The ducklings' home became sacred space in the landscape where real estate is a high commodity.

I was driving a few miles west from my home on a less traveled road, when I saw out of the corner of my eye a brand new floppy eared puppy race out into the road and circle frantically not knowing what to do. I came to a dead stop and rolled down my window while the puppy's young owner looked on in horror from his yard with a face washed over like white chalk. He was dreading the horrible scene getting ready to unfold in living color. He raced out to retrieve the dog, and scooped him up in his arm.

"Thank you, thank you, lady." Relief poured over him, and you could see him relax. I wasn't going to be the culprit.

"Better hang on to him a little better," I said.

"I just got him and I let him go for a second and he ran away so fast I panicked."

Driving off I glanced back out my rear view mirror, and a contented boy was stroking his dog on the side of the road. All was right with his world again.

Coming upon deer season, any veteran of the area knows that his eyes must be roving constantly while driving, and in the most unexpected spots, too. My senses go into mandatory high alert mode.

I've had a daring deer literally fly over the hood of my car sprinting to the other side at the very last second. It's as if we were in a race with a stopwatch counting down. The deer's delicate acrobatics left me shaking like a leaf! I was more than satisfied that the deer won, and I came in a close second.

Small herds of deer habitually cross the road at the bottom of our hill, and I know to slow down giving the landscape an extra scrutiny. The hunters spot them, too, until it is time for the season to begin. Those smarter deer go deeper into the woods playing hide and seek.

When I look up into the sky on many afternoons I catch sight of young eagles circling our area practicing their flying techniques. It seems to me that they are a lot safer off the roads relying on their own traffic control patterns than the rest of us. I envy their great view of the whole earth draped in its colorful seasonal hues.

I never enjoy viewing road kill spread out ahead of me on my travels, although nature has its own way of survival without any interference from me. I will stick to loving the bear, red fox and yes, even the chipmunk, that are my companions on the earth.

For Love and Chocolate

For years and years I have tried to break off a relationship. I rationalized, though, that if I could control myself and minimize my emotions, then I wouldn't feel so guilty.

When I was in Belgium we were introduced, and I have never forgiven my two girl friends for the life-altering occasion. My innocence was lost forever, and I returned home an enlightened woman.

The bottom line: I crave dark chocolate. And I mean good, rich chocolate.

Just how sinful could a bit of chocolate actually be? The Aztecs and the Mayans believed that chocolate transmitted knowledge and power to those who consumed it.

There is a modern day claim to health benefits from eating chocolate in moderation. Well, anything not eaten in excess is my motto. Now, how I would define what "in reasonable limits" means in real caloric intake could become problematic.

Chocolate has been shown to improve your mood by boosting the brain chemical serotonin. You want to be in a good frame of mind, don't you? When the lull of the day is taking its grip on you, a little pick- me- up could pull you over to the happier side of life.

Visiting a store that makes homemade chocolate on the premises is an awesome experience. The sidewalk tugs at you before you open the door to heightened aromas and a panoramic view of delights. You would think that any normal, self-respecting person would not give in to temporary urges. Instead, you should make a mad dash for the other side of the street to other mundane thoughts such as locating a cup of steaming hot cocoa with a swirl of whipped cream.

A person so enamored by chocolate that he becomes an entrepreneur must have a whimsical personality. Does he sneak pieces at random moments while packaging? Or is he like the teen that told me she became sick of ice cream after a single summer scooping at the local stand?

On my last trip to this store I treated myself to dark chocolate with peppermint. Honestly, why I was treating myself, I have no clue. It felt right at the time, and I'll defend my motive. I even had the sales lady wrap it up as a gift with a huge velvety ribbon.

Visiting my grandfather's house as a kid, I would patiently wait for the candy box to circle the room. I would select a piece that I eyeballed while the assortment was passing through hands hoping upon hope that one of my cousins wouldn't use mental telepathy to grab the very piece I wanted before the container reached me.

Around the holidays there was peppermint bark dark chocolate piled high everywhere candy was sold. Selections were flying off the shelves like hotcakes while I stood transfixed. It was as active as a department store lingerie sale table if you know what I mean.

An overzealous shopper, a complete stranger to me, said that she lived for December and her peppermint bark. Now, you'll never hear me making that endorsement. That would be like me saying that I live for reality shows on TV. Maybe that's how she gets through those shows in one piece by nibbling on candy bars.

One of my favorite recipes is a chocolate peppermint bark bar. This is one pure delicious confection that will bring back so many memories. Dark and white chocolate bark is swirled with crushed peppermint candy cane. One bite of this minty chocolate goodness will put a huge smile on the face of the worst Scrooge.

When Valentine's Day arrived in my fourth grade classroom, a boy came up to my desk with a giant heart shaped box. He handed it to me as if it was the most precious gift in the world. In fact, if I can recall correctly, he didn't even take off his coat, but came directly to find me.

Upon opening the lid I saw an assortment of homemade chocolate candies that his mother and him had made together. He proudly stood over me pointing at different samples, and I was impressed. That was a very labor- intensive baking project.

And I felt so honored to receive his thoughtful present. He had chosen to share a little bit of himself with me.

I've been told that chocolate can be an effective diet food. It curbs your appetite if eaten before a meal. Please let the rest of us know if you get positive results.

Wine and chocolate trails have become popular winter weekend events. Skeptics say it cannot be done— pairing wine with chocolate, but if you have the right wine to complement the right chocolate it can be a match made in heaven!

On that trip to Belgium the three of us didn't have too much money, but we did have a big appetite for experiences different from those at home. We took turns daily buying a chocolate bar, and then we would break off sections to feast on walking through the winding streets of Bruges touring magnificent sites.

When it was time to return to the United States during the honeymoon stage of my love affair, my carry-on was carefully packed to the last ounce allowable with gifts of chocolate candy bars for the folks back home. My sticky brownish diary pages were fingered with great memories. The romance would spring eternal.

Share a Closet at Your Own Peril

"His and her" sides of the bedroom closet don't exist according to my husband. He has lost out to female invasiveness like the plague. He accepts that there is no potential cure on the horizon either.

"You own the closet, and I get what tiny space is left over," he complains constantly.

"That's the way it is," I reply back reasonably miffed at his negative attitude. "I have a lot of clothes, and they need to be organized."

"If I leave space for even five minutes, it inevitably disappears."

How we ever got into this mess I don't know. We would be better off trying to solve world hunger, and not allow materialism to creep into our lives.

There's something universal about men muttering that they feel as if they are being hung out to dry along with their modest wardrobes. You would suspect that men believe women control bedroom closet space like inherently they have sole ownership of the TV remote!

"Why do you need so many skirts if you don't teach anymore?"

"You just don't get it." I shake my head in despair.

I take a little offense at being told what should and should not be in my closet. How does my husband know that I might need one of those skirts for an occasion next spring?

"What about all those jackets from your dad that you have stored in the guest bedroom closet? He's been gone for years, and you are not the same size by a long shot."

"So you are telling me if I get rid of them, you will have more space? I don't think so," he retorts shaking his head holding firmly to his stance.

Both of us tossed out suits and "teacher clothes" diligently when we retired, and that wasn't hard at all. They were pretty well worn from the battleground.

Ties from the art room were spattered with clay. One had been shortened unevenly by a good four inches when it got sliced in the paper cutter. What it was being saved for, I have no idea. I decided not to ask. There must have been sentimentality attached to it.

Currently our closet has more casual outfits that fit our present lifestyle. We try to follow a rule that when bringing in something new, out goes an older item. It is hit or miss on whether or not the rule works. The racks keep bulging. There always appears to be wiggle room for another garment in the closet as if the clothing rod is an infinite line in space.

Mindful of others who are in need of clothing, we faithfully purge our closets a couple times a year. For me, it becomes a painful ordeal as I think through each decision. I go back and forth talking to myself, or to any pet that accidently enters the room.

My husband, on the other hand, will often do his cleaning out at a most inopportune moment— like an hour before we are having company come for dinner. You wonder what he is thinking.

However, I should be grateful for small favors. When he sorts it goes at warp speed, and he does a terrific job of elimination. A bag of clothing materializes out of the air like a flash of lightning.

"You're throwing out *that* shirt? You just bought it a couple months ago? I question him with a gleam in my eyes realizing the endless possibilities it has opened up for me.

"It doesn't fit right, and besides I don't ask you to explain what's in your shopping bags when you come home."

None of this sifting through fazes him whatsoever. He has moved on to other projects—hopefully the bathroom floor molding.

Shoes are another matter. I will admit that my collection seems unnecessary to my husband. His theory is you need a couple pairs of everyday shoes, sneakers and a dress pair in the closet. He can't understand how I would need multiple pairs of clogs that match different color schemes.

I have discovered through years of marriage that closet space is a delicate subject between husbands and wives. If you want to liven up a party, try bringing up the subject and see where the conversation leads.

One husband sheepishly told me out of earshot from his wife that his stuff routinely gets shoved to one side.

"No wonder my slacks are wrinkled when I pull them out," he said matter of fact.

As a company executive he doesn't seem like the kind of guy that would stand for such treatment. I am presuming that the spousal arguments have all ironed out through their years of wedded bliss.

I'm not so sure that my single friends don't have closet space issues, as well. I am not going to let them off the hook so easily.

Singles are competing for floor space with their cats and dogs, all their assorted seasonal sports equipment and a pile of nostalgic sweatshirts that are two sizes too small. I would wager a bet that their closet floors are the receptacle for musty, unmatched sneakers along with boxes never opened since moving in.

Tonight my husband and I will hang out together and agree to a compromise. It's the beginning of a new year after all. When all is said and done, may it lean heavily to my side of the hangers!

Dancing in My Dreams with Dick Clark

I slow danced alone without guilt. And it wasn't once either. It was a regular late afternoon ritual in the living room. The black and white console TV was tuned to Dick Clark's American Bandstand.

Dick Clark was my date. He was an icon and was referred to as "the oldest teenager in America."

Back in the 50s, WFIL-TV in Philadelphia needed a replacement show for its movie time slot. A new concept in broadcasting emerged. A rotating group of area high schoolers were invited to dance on the show with a few regulars to the latest countdown of popular singles. Cameras panned in and out among the dancers. Clark would interview a special guest before the performer would lip-sync to his vinyl 45 spinning on the turntable.

Under Clark, American Bandstand became the longest running variety show from 1957-1987. In fact, his show became the forerunner of the music video so familiar today.

Fast rock 'n roll twists and turns spun me around cushioned by the green shag carpet. Slow strolls and dreamy love music glided me into a shadowy corner out of sight of my mother in the kitchen. I could do all the steps with the energy of a spirited girl free of a long day of high school classes. I was a natural, and I loved to dance.

Clark truly legitimized rock 'n roll to adults making it a viable music art form. Up until then, it was a teenage craze that parents wished would go away.

Ike and Tina Turner, Stevie Wonder and Simon and Garfunkel got their first exposure on American Bandstand. Their careers were launched and they went on to stardom.

By second period high school chemistry class, where I was a hopeless loser, my mind blotted out the equations and focused on racing home to Dick Clark. It was a fine balance. I hoped upon hope that nothing would deter me from making it through the backdoor in time for the opening of the show, the screaming teens on the floor waiting for the camera to roll and Dick Clark's appearance.

Paul Anka was my fantasy heartthrob. What a voice! What looks! He had it made thanks to Dick Clark's showcase for fledging talent. When Anka crooned, "Put Your Head on My Shoulder," I wrapped my crossed arms together over my chest and closed my eyes. I kissed my shoulder and dreamed of the boy who sat behind me in band. Would he ever ask me out?

Dick Clark had the first venue where African Americans and whites performed and danced on the same stage. He appeared to get it right with all people regardless of ethnicity.

A popular portion of the show was when Clark interviewed teens. He asked for their opinions on the hit songs. In the "Rate a Record" segment, teens would give the record a number. "It's got a good beat and you can dance to it." Clark would average the marks before asking the audience to judge. Many a brand new song rose in popularity on the radio immediately after that afternoon session. It was a great marketing tool asking youth to endorse products.

I told all my secrets and wildest dreams to Dick Clark. He knew that I was making plans after high school to go to flight stewardess school in New York. I was one-half inch shorter than the minimum requirement, and I reasoned that stretching and dancing would help me grow. I would lie on the floor and my little sister would be called in to extend first my legs and then my arms as hard as she could pull. It never got me anywhere, but I tried for Dick Clark.

Certain afternoons my friends and I were together at one of our homes. Still we danced the fast dances alone, and kept to our separate corners for the slow dances. We talked for hours and we would copycat the hairstyles and outfits of the dancers to perfection. Our dream was to skip school on Long Island and hitchhike to Philly to be on the show. Somehow that never materialized, and I suppose our parents never knew of our plan— or did they?

Throughout the decades Clark rang in new years for us to celebrate like clockwork. Generations knew him by his voice alone and his relaxed manner. Perhaps that is what kept him looking so youthful. He brought vibrancy and a joy of life through the post World War II era of prosperity and the confusing Vietnam period. We all suffered with him after his major stroke, and cheered for his slow deliberate recovery. Although Clark never quite made the mark again physically, he was a fighter.

Dick Clark put his seal of approval on my early growing up period. I was vocalizing my own melody, not quite in harmony with the adult world yet. Thanks, Dick Clark. This dance is for you: "You are my Destiny."

Dining off the Beaten Path Presents Challenges

There are those of you that can size-up an unfamiliar place from the outside. You have a hunch and think nothing of going inside.

If you've watched Guy Fieri on "Diners, Drive-ins and Dives" and followed his madcap adventures, the thrill of the quest might pay off with an outstanding eating experience. Then again, it might be one to wipe off your plate.

Opening the front door to a small town restaurant puts you in uncharted territory. Its not one of those activities for the faint of heart, or the "picky" eater.

My husband and I have noticed that eateries that dot along the highways and towns of America offer down home cooking, and in other cases, overwhelm you with gourmet meals rivaling any urban establishment. We pull over and take advantage of the invitation. You just never know.

Those funky little joints have been etched in our minds forever with stories and pictures to share with the folks at home. Often, others will pick up on our suggestions and return with their own versions.

There are plenty of chains up and down the route for those who thrive on the comfort of the familiar in life. Sometimes it might be the best choice, too, or the only one handy.

We had been eating our way through southern New Mexico one winter following the travel guide's recommendations. Normally we don't tie ourselves to a guidebook and leave a length of rope for the twists of spontaneity to encircle us. However, we decided to play the tourist role up to the hilt.

A late afternoon arrived and we went on a road trip south from Las Cruces to a Mexican restaurant that the travel guide recommended. "A place with tasty food in an authentic atmosphere," the hefty book told us.

We drove surrounded by beautiful vistas. It was quite a hike from the city, and we assumed that this must be quite the special place to warrant the guide's three-star rating.

Whoa! We pulled up to a dilapidated doublewide building on the edge of an unpaved parking lot that looked more like a roadside bar. A haphazard collection of beat up pick-ups was parked near the sole shade tree. The only sign of life was a couple stray dogs that came out to greet us. They quickly went on their way foraging for food.

I double–checked the guidebook to make sure that this was in fact the local haunt that the book claimed, "a must eat at before leaving New Mexico." Yes, the tumbledown place was right in front of us.

We did that "should we, or shouldn't we routine" couples are so good at playing off each other. Somebody had to take the lead, and my husband stepped up making the final decision. We hesitantly went up to the doorway where we heard a hum of conversation and a clinking of glasses from within.

My husband walked through the swinging doorway gallantly and I was right behind him. Suddenly the place came to a standstill, and what I feared the most was right in front of me. The look on my face was worth a thousand pictures he told me later.

A dimly lit saloon right out of a vintage western movie was straight ahead. Half a dozen cowboys donned in their working garb and wide brimmed hats turned in unison to stare at us.

All I saw was guns in their holsters and spurs on their boots before my head dropped to avert their eyes.

Not knowing our surroundings and already committed, we couldn't make a quick getaway... no matter how fast the horse. That didn't seem like a very smart notion at all. We timidly tip toed over the rough- hewn boards and took corner seats. I felt my bodily heat rising by the second, and my trembling weak legs were grateful to hide behind a table.

We'd been noticed. Word would get out. How soon before the sheriff would come riding up to escort us out of Dodge?

Obviously, we had gotten the wrong place.

Time stood still before the barmaid eventually sauntered over. A little liquid refreshment and a bowl of nachos hit the spot while we plotted our escape concerned about our safety. It was written all over our faces, and not from the hot sauce either. You can guess who would get blamed for this escapade back at the motel!

The cowboys went back to their business, dismissing the city slickers as has been the habit of cowboys since they came to be. They left us alone.

When the bartender came back to refill our glasses we asked if they served meals. That's when we found out that the actual restaurant was a little room off to the side with its own private entrance. All our apprehensions could have been avoided.

Soon the local crowd started filling the three or four other tables. They nodded. By then we were acclimated enough to have a delicious dinner in the bar.

The guidebook was right on! It's too bad they didn't give a little forewarning about leaving your nerves at home.

Since then on our journeys, we have opened the door to many mom and pop eating spots. None will ever compare to our initial entry into everyday life in the Wild West.

When we got up to leave, all the cowboys turned around together and smiled at us. Now that was wicked cool!

Off we galloped into the New Mexico sunset leaving a cloud of dust behind us.

The Presence of Children Keeps Adults Younger

Wherever kids are found there will be noisy restless bodies in every size and shape. There is no getting around it. It is a fact of life—precious young life.

Others don't agree necessarily. The further removed from kids and grandkids by age, the more annoying children are to them.

There are outstanding lessons to be learned from little kids if you are willing to give it a chance.

There was quite a stir on social media sites last year when a restaurant would not allow children under the age of six to dine. Chatter was a flutter with opinions right and left of the fork.

Mike Vuick, owner of McDain's Restaurant and Golf Center in Monroeville, Pa., took a stand. He was quoted in newspapers all over the country in July 2011.Vuick said that he was doing this on behalf of all the kind, refined people who had emailed him about ruined meals. He decided someone in society had to dig in his heels.

It is inevitable with kids that meltdowns come with their little psyches. Frequently it happens at the most inopportune time. Those cherubim wings have been left behind in the van to reattach during snooze time on the way home. That's the nature of growing up. Observers can be sympathetic or downright nasty.

In public places parents fret at their lack of control skills. It leaves them in a tizzy and in desperate need of affirmation from friends and family who have wisdom to impart. Sometimes the kindly words from a stranger right on the scene can be reassuring, too.

I get my feathers ruffled when those around me complain about kids in certain settings. You wonder about their personal issues that bring out their negativity with everything within range. It's all in how parents deal with their kids that makes or breaks the deal.

Having a bad day? Down in the dumps? There is nothing like going to a kid zone—a fast food establishment, a G movie or a kid- climbing zoo to boost your spirits, though.

The laughter and natural freedom to take risks and experiment is so pervasive. What delight to watch kids connecting with other tykes and tackling a slide, or each other?

A lot of life's lessons about getting along start on the playground. It might be a good reminder to phone someone, laugh a bit more at everyday things and stay active physically.

As adults we are so controlling and directive. The clock is ticking and life's calendar forces us onward. Oh, the liberation a little one has to appreciate his surroundings.

Watch a two year old on the playground that has spotted a ladybug crawling over his shoe. How long will they just look at each other while the toddler takes in the wonder of the colors, textures and sense of togetherness with nature? The wheels are turning in his head.

Everyone is aware that a successful fishing trip can't be rushed. Help a little one learn to fish and you will have a companion for life! Whether it is at a special catch and release pond where training is in session, or a good old-fashioned stream nearby, there are opportunities for the asking.

"We wind the grandkids up and send them home." Grandparents are alike everywhere. It's at grandma's house where the kids get the heaping bowl of ice cream not once, but twice in a day. And grandma places no limits on how many chocolate chip cookies (because she said it was okay) with a wink of her eye.

I love it when a preschooler asks me if I would read him a story. Suddenly a stack of favorite, worn books materialize from the bedroom. I am on my honor to read exactly what's on the page with no skipping of pages allowed—no, not a single sentence. Those are the (unwritten) rules. Otherwise, do I get reminded in no uncertain terms!

Dr. Seuss has his way with words, and those sayings are crucial to a little emergent reader. There is comfort in hearing the familiar phrases when mom is away and someone else is taking up the slack.

Years ago Art Linkletter wrote a book, "Kids Say the Darndest Things," based on an early television show where he interviewed children. Of course, the answers were clever and cute. Viewers were awed. You have to remember that this was during a period when kids were beginning to be heard instead of silenced in an adult world. Today, whether or not a show like that would work is a different matter. Kids pretty much say it like it is.

Still out of the mouths of babes can be some really prophetic and choice words to make adults chuckle! Kids are perfectly honest, too. That might prove to be a good lesson for adults to live by instead of dancing around things that should be said to one another.

The next time you see a kid collapsing on an escalator refusing to move upon the command of his dad, let it go. When you see a kid bouncing from under the clothes rack in the department store playing hide and seek with his mom, let it go. The next generation of inquisitive minds is being developed right underfoot.

Appreciate young children for all they are worth. Run away with a fresh spirit instead of stomping down in irritation.

If Less is Enough, Then How Much Do I Need?

In the middle of the pharmaceutical aisle at the grocery store I became overwhelmed with all the choices that I had available to remedy a simple head cold.

I completely came to a grinding halt. When I starting looking up and down the shelves to find something that would cure the nasty germ that was shutting me down, I didn't know what to do. Thanks to too many companies eager for my business, I was in a frenzied indecisiveness.

Always one to carefully read labels, I had plenty of those to study just to figure out if I wanted a pill, capsule or jell. When I reached out for one and examined it, it went back on the shelf because I don't do ones that make me drowsy.

The way it was shaping up it appeared that I would need both a daytime and night time tablet, along with cough medicine and drops for my throat. I was not going to leave without dropping a pretty penny.

Well, you get it. It was endless. Fortunately, the pharmacist came over noticing I was going into meltdown mode, and she picked out a couple products that I put into my cart. By then I didn't care anymore as long as it cleared up my sniffles.

Too many choices had demotivated me—or was it unmotivated me? See how I had become so exhausted from logical thinking that I was befuddled and mismanaging language?

Since I wasn't feeling up to par, I hurriedly finished my shopping with some haphazard aisle skipping hoping to avoid a familiar face.

When I got to the diaper aisle—I didn't need any of those, I spotted a young mom with one of those carts that carries two toddlers in pre-driver training, plus a baby up top. She looked very put together for having three little ones, and she was calmly checking her coupons against the products on the shelves.

"How many types do you need?" I asked her as she pulled packages off the shelf systematically filling in the spaces around the babies.

"I have one in training panties, a night-timer and an infant," she laughed.

There it was again—that feeling of less might be more than enough. Our society has us all so conditioned to expect too many options for everything. Back in the day the options were limited. What was wrong with cloth diapers? I danced away from that aisle befuddled, blowing my nose profusely and wanting to get home to the couch.

Shortly I got a call from a young thirty something friend who told me about her recent saga finding the perfect man for her life.

"How's it coming?" I wanted to give her all the encouragement that I could for the task she had ahead.

"I'm into speed dating [a generic name for SpeedDating™] and I am meeting new men without investing a lot of wasted dates on ones that don't work."

If you are not up to speed, let me say that basically it is a formalized event where people gather and do round robin socializing in three to eight minute segments to find out if they are romantically attracted to each other. At the end of the evening everyone gives the organizers a list of those that they want to share their contact information.

I went online—where else, to check out speed dating, and I discovered that you are able do it from your computer without leaving the privacy of your home or office, too. For some people the bar scene doesn't cut it, and their free time is so limited with work travel.

I suppose then that in our hurried world speed dating fits with the philosophy of less time is all you need to find the right person. It made me think about how long it took for me to decide whether my husband was the one for me. Could it have been between the three to eight minute time frame as we drove off on our first date?

Yep. I believe it was so, with the "ah-ha" moment right between my house and the top of the hill.

Furthermore, I recollect that I knew in a very short time that it was going to be a go for life. In our case, it was a set-up blind date, too. My husband invited me out on a weeknight thinking if the date went "south" he wouldn't have ruined a weekend. I guess he got fooled totally! So, here again, less may be more than enough if you intuitively know yourself and where you are headed.

Women tend to require friendships with a lot more contact between them than men do. Some even get extremely paranoid if the other has multiple friends, or one goes off for a while in other directions.

My husband and his childhood best friend infrequently see each other, but when they do, it appears that they continue on where they left off. Less works for them, and is more than enough.

A close friend wisely said, "Less contact does not mean less love," giving me a whole new take on friendship that I was never able to envision before. That philosophy could lead to more honest, caring relationships that last a lifetime.

Perhaps, more than enough is less in some people's eyes. Less in my eyes is more than I could ever hope to achieve.

A Thank You From France: Sealed with a Kiss

Everything about the Notre Dame Church, the focal point for the Mantes-la-Jolie community in the Normandy region of France, is magnificent from its towering arches to its saintly statues.

Dating from the end of the 12th century, the church has stood proudly through history, after the original church was burned down by William the Conqueror in 1087 during a siege on the town that cost him his life. It was rebuilt. More recently, the church remained intact while surrounding buildings were reduced to rubble after bombing raids in World War II.

It was in the narthex of the cathedral that my husband had an encounter that will remain with us to this day. As he was examining the old photographs depicting the devastation, a sturdy woman in a navy cloth coat purposefully walked up to him and started talking animatedly in French, of course, but to no avail as neither he nor I could pick out more than one or two words. Yet the words that we *did* hear—"*résistance* and *liberté*" —were part of what she was trying to say.

"You are thanking Americans for liberating you?" guessed my husband.

"Oui!" she exclaimed.

Apologizing to her in English (with some desperate sign language thrown in), we could do no more. We started out the door to meet up with our tour guide and the rest of the group, but she followed us with a determined look on her face. She marched right up to our guide and initiated a lively conversation. At first puzzled, he regained his thoughts and began translating her message.

This lovely angelic looking lady told us how much she appreciated what the U.S. armed forces had done for France. She explained that she had not had bread for several years during the German occupation, and her first slice was from a loaf of American white bread.

"Merci. Merci." She nodded her head over and over.

She clasped her hands together and clapped to all of us spanning the entire group. As if that was not enough, she blew a kiss.

What a moment of gratitude as she stood on the steps of a hospital that had been rebuilt after it was bombed during the war within a hundred yards of the church. As quickly as she had appeared, she walked off across the street head held high.

We had never even thought to ask her name. There wasn't a sound uttered. We were simply stunned.

Our tour guide had tears in his eyes when he explained that it isn't uncommon to run into appreciative older people who lived through all the hardships of war. Although the younger generation (like him) had heard the stories, here was a person that had lived it firsthand reminding us of our mutual history.

Later my husband and I discussed what had unfolded while having an espresso in a local café.

"She had the same view of America as I have. We are good people, and do good things," commented my husband. " In recent years we have heard a lot about how we as Americans try to impose our way of life on others."

Two strangers met in a church and cultures crossed briefly. That is the beauty of travel: not the food, sights nor the museums, (although they have their value), but a discovery when you are least expecting it. What truly leaves a lasting memory is the moment you have connected with a fellow human being—no matter how brief.

I Cast My Ballot for Lima Beans

The other day I was galloping down the canned fruits and vegetable aisle at the grocery store. There were worldly thoughts swirling in my mind, and I was occupied. However, when my eyes zeroed in on the lima bean section, I re-entered reality.

Suddenly a rush of nostalgia waved over me. I grabbed a can, put it lovingly in my cart and sighed right then and there. I don't know what came over me.

Lima beans must have been the childhood comfort food I needed. Whether or not it would compliment peppers stuffed with bison for the evening meal didn't much matter. My mood elevated. My feet trotted faster swinging the cart aggressively into the next row.

Living in a part of the country where fresh fruits and vegetables abound, I lean heavily on them and infrequently pick up frozen packages or cans. I am programmed to eating locally, regionally, as well as seasonally. It's a great adventure to go to area farmers' markets, and see what is heaped on the tables or on the backs of pick- up trucks directly from fields and gardens. Like everyone else though, I do stock up on those cans and frozen packages for emergencies. I never know who might be coming for dinner, or what ingredient could be missing from a recipe in progress.

After checking out at the counter and stuffing my recyclable bags into the trunk of my car, I couldn't contain myself. It was a momentous opportunity right in front of me. I began to imagine what memory those lima beans had triggered.

"Eat your vegetables."

"Clean your plate."

"Children are starving in Africa."

That's what I heard ringing like hourly chimes on a clock. All those universal threats and coercive forces parents pull out to use during desperate times pushed to the forefront.

Fortunately, I did like to eat pretty much everything as a kid, and my weight stayed manageable with help from a lot of outside play. Apparently, "mealtime badgering" didn't traumatize me.

That's not the case with everybody, though. I talked to one mother who told me that she hated certain vegetables growing up. She remembered choking down lima beans, Brussels sprouts and peas. Meals were extremely unpleasant. She decided that as a parent she wouldn't force her kids to eat them.

"Food does not have to be a battle. There are plenty of other healthy choices."

I wholeheartedly agree. I too, sat watching a tiny daughter twirling vegetables around on her plate like an ice skater until I got smart about it. A change in my attitude and tactics worked wonders.

Selecting a couple dozen people, I administered an unscientific poll. There seemed to be an all out either "love 'em or hate 'em" relationship with the edible, whitish bean that first made its presence known in Peru.

Folks were emphatic; we must clarify which bean we were in conversation about— baby lima beans, or regular lima beans.

Someone told me that they liked lima beans plain, in succotash and in the "mystery casserole" at the potluck church dinner.

Ah, succotash brought many comments. One friend replied that when mom's "vegetable medley" appeared at dinnertime, he had his work cut out for him carefully scooping out everything else to avoid the beans. That took an artful slight of the hand to keep the grown-ups from seeing what was transpiring.

"Maybe it was the unique taste combo of the limas and the corn that did it for me; or the cool yellow and green color of the two veggies," said one volunteer readily answering my question. Why, I can see her serving up beans for dinner tonight!

My sister was a puny eater. She would slip the beans into her napkin one at a time, and scurry from the table when she could make an exit while I was monopolizing our parents with an unreasonable request. She knew how to play the game well. Where did she stash her little treasures? Since she loved tea parties with her dollies, I would guess that they were served on a platter along with stale breadcrumbs.

Southern friends were raised on a staple of dried beans, butter beans, lima beans and pintos. When I head to those states I might as well face up to assorted bean dishes at every meal like it or not.

Lima beans cooked with bacon were a fond memory for a friend stationed in Jacksonville, North Carolina. Someone in his barracks invited him home, and between a little Southern hospitality to a Northern boy far from New York State, and those drippings of fat on his beans, he won't ever forget that experience.

My husband and I pondered about lima beans as we sat down to the stuffed pepper meal that evening.

"Why do you suppose we had so many meals that included canned or frozen lima beans when we were kids? Was it cheap, plentiful, or both?"

Considering the amount of shelving space allotted to lima beans at the grocery store, they might have never left us.

Hey, those pesky, stick-on-your teeth skins might prove the next best thing for hygienists promoting mouthwash, floss and cleaning. Certainly no politician wants to tackle smiles with a lowly lima bean stuck in his mouth during the up-coming political campaign.

Move over broccoli. I am going way out on a beanpole and predicting that lima beans will become the new comeback veggie for the next ten years.

Hear! Hear!

Not a Pure Leftie or a Right-handed Woman

Multiple bees stung me on my right hand. Bee bummer. Ouch!

I have myself to blame for stupidity, though. I should have put on gardening gloves before reaching in to a flowerbed to pull out a clump of weeds. It was one of those deals where I was passing by in a hurry and didn't realize that I would be out in the yard so long. I got carried away in my excitement of yanking and pulling nuisances from the ground. You would think I had better sense at my age.

Of course, my hand got swollen and looked dreadful. An herbalist gave me a salve to use and after a night of throbbing the situation appeared somewhat better. Still my hand was dysfunctional. I looked like a Star Trek voyager unable to power up all systems for a "go."

Which leads me to being thankful that I am left-handed. Hold on. Not so fast. Well, actually I am ambidextrous, making me all the more confusing to be seen with in public! I eat, play ball, knit with my right hand, and almost write legibly with my right hand, too. How did I ever get as far in life as I have under those conditions?

So I write best with my left-hand, and that is the one I use primarily. I was a real problem child for my first grade teacher, though, as in the old Palmer Method, I could never get the mirrored effect right. My slant was off and it didn't feel natural to my touch. The shadow of my teacher hovering over me with a scowl on her face is one I can see today. I am sure she thought that I was hopeless with my crooked slash marks on the wide ruled paper.

In other words, traditional elementary school penmanship class was a nightmare for me. Society valued handwriting, and it was such a big deal, too. Here's the kicker: When I became a teacher I was overly sympathetic to fellow lefties. A few students told me it was the first time in their elementary years that a teacher got it. That must have been a relief for them.

When I started teacher training I further exasperated my professors. Before they would even let me go into a campus school setting to practice my teaching skills I had to have acceptable penmanship with a proper slant to the right. Knowing in my heart that I loved teaching and it was the career for me, the only way I was to get out of the program was to train myself to write. I did. It must have worked. In fact, one of my former second grade students remembers me for my beautiful penmanship to this very day! Bless her!

Later on everything relaxed, including my handwriting when I taught higher grades. Enter computers into the world and it was even better. I am not sure what it has done for children's cursive abilities. I see that many do a combo of printing and cursive with little skill to it. I hear a lot of grandparents complaining that handwriting is no longer an art.

To look at my handwriting today you would shake your head. It's gone to the dogs. I do most of my writing on the computer. I met someone several years ago and I don't think that we have actually seen each other's handwriting —not that we need it to analyze one another to maintain our friendship.

I love reading how left-handed people are considered more creative and less conventional. Right the experts are, except when you are learning a new sport such as golf. I reluctantly signed up for lessons with the golf pro, and I was dreading the first lesson. As in most sports when you are a leftie, the coach says to think of the move in the opposite direction and you will be all set. The burden gets placed on me; I am stuck trying every which way to figure it out. Not this pro, though. He turned around, picked up my left-handed golf club to show me how to swing. He shot a very decent ball for being a right-hander. That was so great for me. I caught on rather easily after that.

A kindhearted lady taught me how to knit the German way, and it was simple until as I got more advanced and wanted to do patterns. I had to trace each one painstakingly. I was wrapping the yarn over my left needle. A friend with the patience of Job started me from scratch in adulthood knitting right-handed. I guess I should be glad for the flexible quality to my brain.

Don't get me going on the uselessness of left-handed scissors. I have never gotten the knack for using them, and will cut with my right hand.

I pick up a fork with whichever hand pleases me at the moment, although my parents trained me to eat right-handed. I defiantly grabbed a pencil to print my name with my left hand and that sole event marked my personality from that day forward according to my mother.

In living life I have come to buckle up, full speed ahead with a firm grip on reality. Resistance is futile.

My Special Shangri- la Calls Me Softly

I picked up a rock from the Mojave Desert and carefully examined it. Ah…I felt as if I had returned to where I belong.

The desert always has held a fascination for me. It is a place that speaks deeply to my soul, and I am sensitive to the creativity that flows from me as a result.

It is a painter's delight with its minimal landscape and gorgeous sky. No wonder artists like Georgia O'Keeffe have immortalized the starkness and beauty in powerful work. Her white canvasses with simple flowers sparkle intensely.

My Texas Panhandle friend, a watercolorist, has permitted the freedom of a large sky to open up and loosen her style with a softer palette. It's so different from when she resided in the East painting the wintry hills.

Looking at one of her pieces I take in the hugeness and unstructured qualities of the desert down to the solitary ball of tumbleweed blowing in the wind. The message expressed is of a wide-open space mentality that makes one rugged and fiercely independent.

She lives that way, too, and her western style is a natural extension of her art. The cowboy boots, shimmering turquoise jewelry and brightly flowing skirts are part of the costume of the environment that she wears so elegantly.

The New Mexico lavender sunsets are the most awesome wonders every night, and I will stop whatever I am doing—even a good dinner with friends, to observe all the subtleties of the tints and hues crossing the horizons. The unique displays never disappoint night after night.

Once I purposely made plane reservations in order to land in Albuquerque late in the afternoon with enough time to head out west of the city to a quiet rural area to sit and observe the free feature on the screen surrounding me. Others were parked here and there along the roadside, too. Whatever their motives, folks were tuned to nature's spectacle deep in their own thoughts.

As often as I have tried to capture all this natural beauty with my camera, it is the vivid memory of the sky that lingers much better.

Writers, too, have found solace and expression in the quietness in the air.

"For all the toll that the desert takes of a man, it gives compensations, deep breaths, deep sleep, and the communion of the stars," said Mary Austin in "The Land of Little Rain."

It doesn't take me long to let my mind wander and gather ideas together to put down in my journal or laptop nowadays. Sometimes I am in much better form than in any other place, and I can work without any interruption getting down to the bones of a piece.

Standing and staring for miles and miles ahead with nothing to distract me is soothing and spiritual in a personal way, too.

It happened by chance that I was vacationing in the Southwest when 9/11 occurred, and once I was satisfied that my Manhattan friends and family were safe, I immediately was pulled to the desert to think things through. Scanning for miles with nothing in sight was the remedy that I needed. Since planes were grounded there was nowhere to go anyhow. I did feel far away from home. The landscape was such a sharp contrast to densely populated Manhattan swirling in havoc and confusion.

By that Friday when I drove through a small town in southern Utah and saw the chain link fence at the local school covered with woven red, white and blue crepe paper flags, I realized that all Americans collectively were mourning. That was comforting.

How ironic that I was in a desert environment when another major event in world history occurred with the death of Osama Bin Laden in Pakistan. Again, the urge to be outdoors wrapped in the desert forced me to slow down enough to absorb the fast-paced news story evolving by the minute.

The first time that I ever went to the desert I arrived on a late night plane into Tucson. I sure was in for a surprise the next morning as I drove through the open countryside! I couldn't believe the saguaros of various shapes and sizes right in people's yards. The unique desert landscaping made each home worth gawking over.

Driving on further it became too much for me to comprehend. I paused just to clear out my eastern head of rainy notions and soak in the sunshine that the local Arizona weatherman made no big deal over. Apparently, it would be sunny, sunny and sunny every day no matter in which direction I turned.

I occasionally contemplate that if I were to move to a desert region would I be as satisfied as a resident, or would I start taking it all for granted not appreciating what I love so much? Would dry skin, the fickle afternoon winds and the excessive summer heat get to me?

It never fails but about the very same time, something or someone new enters my life at home and things change in a different direction erasing those thoughts temporarily.

I know that I will return to the desert, and I will be just as excited as on my initial discovery. I will throw my hands up into the air and shout for joy once again. It's inevitable.

Posting My Vote on Social Networking

I will make no apologies for my love of social networking, particularly on Facebook.

My friendly nature has kept me in contact with others all my life whether it has been by handwritten letters—perish the thought these days, or phone calls. Now with texting, emailing and live online chats, I am putting it to optimal use.

There are varying opinions about shedding one's privacy, and I am willing to listen to what the experts have to say, but as for me, I am not going to shrink away from networking. If anything, I want to put the latest technology to work for me.

I can assure you that I take the necessary precautions with the privacy settings on Facebook, and I never announce my entire comings and goings either. If you want to look me up, you won't find much about me from my public profile. Besides, I have to "friend" you before you are able to see the whole enchilada of my doings.

What I write on my page reflects who I am as a person, and I will leave the nasty, vulgar comments to others—and those people I can block, from coming up on my news feed. Hopefully, I post thought-provoking statements that entice my friends to add their opinions on a subject leaving a long thread of conversation.

What does disturb me, though, is reading posts from someone who is putting his whole life out there for others to see, including sharing with his virtual friends that his girlfriend is having an affair. Or worse yet, all the life that he does appear to have is wrapped up in saying "good night" on Facebook every evening. I can pick out the needy people from the happy, secure people on Facebook after reading a few comments.

I have had some heartwarming experiences in my estimation that have proven worthwhile for me to be on Facebook.

Take for example, a "connect" that I made from someone in California that recognized my maiden name and contacted me via a private message. We started back and forth with short notes, but soon we got so excited about "finding" each other that we went to the telephone to continue our conversation. After hearing each other's voices we laughed over which one of us still sounded more like a native Long Islander than the other.

It turned out that we both grew up on the opposite ends of the same street, and with his steel-trap mind he remembered all sorts of details that I had long ago buried. Actually, he has become a living reference book for the neighborhood, and I have been begging him to write it down.

He told me about visiting my dad's linen store as a young boy of seven and having just enough money to buy his grandmother an embroidered handkerchief for her birthday. You see his mother had passed away when he was very young, and his grandmother was raising him.

My dad knew this, and probably everything else about people living in a small town, which he carefully did not share at home with my sister and me at the time for obvious reasons.

My friend told me how dad treated him like any other adult customer buying a gift. He looked and looked at all the choices on the long center table before selecting one with just the right amount of lace around the edges. He knew not to touch, but he said that it was hard to keep his hands in his pockets along with his roll of quarters. Dad made a big deal over the purchase and he wrapped the handkerchief in a gift box with a lovely bow.

He never forgot that kindness at a point in life when he needed it as an impressionable young boy. Later on he wondered if he actually had enough money, or possibly, dad took what he had and left it at that. His grandmother and my father have since passed away, but we shared a special moment over that story because of Facebook. Each of us shed a tear or two with gratitude for our families.

On one of our trips to California my husband and I will meet my hometown friend at his place of work in the public relations department at Disneyland, and talk more about our good life growing up in a small town.

After that episode, the whole Facebook connect thing just mushroomed, and before you knew it I had "friended" the others that grew up on Lincoln Street, too, around the same time period. We were raised when all ages played ball together, performed in backyard makeshift circuses and even challenged one another to board games. Each of us brings a different slant on our early childhood into our conversations, and those good memories bond us together.

Getting ambitious one day, I started a group alumni page for my beloved elementary school, and now I have many more contacts from not only the neighborhood, but from all over town.

Facebook is an efficient way for keeping up with my social contacts, sending quick birthday greetings and not loosing touch with former colleagues. I love the surprise contacts from people who enrich my life simply by reaching out.

Now that's 21st century!

Staying in Your Lane

Watching junior swimmers splash their arms and legs like crazy in a short race at the local pool keeps the coach just as energized cheering them on from the sideline.

"Stay in your lane," he yells clapping his hands together enthusiastically while he paces back and forth.

There's a lot more jumping up and down from the parents in the stands while the race is ending. The cheerful winner is recognized with a small trophy, and hopefully, a photo in the local newspaper.

Now will come more lessons from the coach, innumerable swimming meets and eventually one or two of the kids will move on to the next level of competition.

That "staying in your lane" philosophy makes plenty of sense to me, and I would say that it has kept me moving forward. I've had to deal with more than a few detours in life before getting on the path again, but I won't complain.

I don't like it when my GPS says, "recalculating." Obviously it is nudging me back on the designated route.

A Facebook friend told me, "Everyone has their own path through life. It was forged especially for you and you alone. Avoid following another's path, as it will only lead to heartache. Sometimes one's lane will parallel another and in that you will find happiness. Avoid stepping into an oncoming lane. As it will always result in a collision."

In his twenties my father was a professional lifeguard in Brooklyn, and his swimming ability remained unparalleled way into his later years. His style was an art form. He swam like he was meant to live in the water. I would marvel at how he could glide effortlessly for what seemed likes ages with a solid stroke that barely set out a ripple. His breathing was very deep and calm, too.

Dad tried to teach me to carry on a conversation while swimming. He wanted me to slow me down and keep relaxed while going for the distance. Usually I could make it just so far, and I would give up treading water while dad swam further.

I realize that is how my dad led his life, too. He had a lot of stamina and determination; he stayed on course always doing the best that he could.

From the outside it would appear that life was effortless for him and that his success as a businessman was natural. It wasn't though, because I saw all the hard work that went along with owning a store that took his total involvement.

A few years ago when I went "over the pond" to visit a friend who was on a teaching exchange in Holland, I got the shock of my lifetime experiencing the German Autobahn firsthand!

"Kay, you take the backseat. You will be better off there," said my wise driver friend who was experienced in high-speed travel.

Sure enough, what little I could see of the scenery was enough along with jetlag and lack of food in my stomach from the overnight flight.

Sometimes life, too, is fast, high risked and requires quick decision making. One must stay focused and on top of his game plan.

My brother-in-law bought a cute Alfa Romeo when my sister and him lived outside London. When I came to visit she was in the process of not only reviewing her rusty stick shift skills, but also learning to drive on the left-hand side of the road. In the two-seater, my brake foot was continually jamming the floor while my sister wove us in and around tight curves on narrow country roads.

There is no room to be tentative about life and its opportunities. There is room for learning curves along the way, however.

A young friend tells me, "Every time something is planned, no matter what it is, there is a beginning point and an end. Take the direct route that was planned. It doesn't allow for detours, distractions and other exits along the way. It's a very focused result- driven way of staying on task from the beginning to the end."

Families that raise mentally or physically challenged children know exactly how important structure is for their child -rearing with stated beginnings and endings. Step-by-step advances and tiny achievements are priceless to them, and they all deserve accolades for staying in their lanes.

All this drives me to a big point about staying in my lane, and I mean it in the literal sense of keeping between the lines on the pavement.

Road warriors that are texting and cell phoning that weave off their lane and into mine are a hazard! I suppose that in the scheme of things that the police have to deal with daily, this is a minor infraction. I beg to differ.

Oh, I have had my share of incidences lately, and it reminds me that it isn't always me, but the other driver that I need to watch out for constantly. I am my brother's keeper, and staying in my lane, or out of the way so someone can pass by is part of what life is all about. It has nothing to do with fairness. I'll get to my destination all in due time.

Perhaps it is best for me to stay in my lane and tread water occasionally. More importantly, I will refocus beyond the horizon and kick-off with renewed vigor when I get the signal.

Strategic Planning Required
Before a Visit to the Vet

Our cat, Dickens, made his annual pilgrimage to the vet's office. For a peanut weighing in at 12 pounds, he rules the roost at our house I'm ashamed to admit. He makes two grown adults beckon at his every command. Mind you, these are the same two people who disciplined hundreds of kids at school successfully for years, raised a child and engaged with numerous other nieces, nephews and assorted pets.

Being an independent guy who comes and goes as he pleases through his special cat door, it is a major strategic lesson preparing to get Dickens crated the morning of the ride down the hill. You'd think we were preparing a military exercise for combat battle.

The night before, my husband gets the cat crate into the guest bathroom and hidden in the shower. The rationale is that it will be easier to contain Dickens in a small room, and less chance for him to play the escape artist living up to his name. We are also assuming that Dickens has no curiosity whatsoever, and during the night, in his rounds of the house, he will not spot the crate.

"Now here's what we will do. You are not going to get hyper, but keep calm and stick with the plan," says my husband, the lead strategist.

"Since when do I get hyper?" I retort selecting my matched camouflage outfit for the early morning maneuver.

"When Dickens saunters into the kitchen for his breakfast in the morning, I will pick him up. DO NOT yell or scream. Just follow me into the bathroom and shut the door behind me."

"OK. And what if he jumps out of your arms on the way to the bathroom?"

"DO NOT yell or scream. I will handle this."

The next morning when Dickens comes to sit on my lap for a few moments of petting and ear rubbing my husband is not in his agreed upon position dressed in his combat uniform ready to intercept. He is still in the shower. Dickens hops down off my lap, strolls over to his feeding dish and then looks up at me as if to say, "Get out of my way. I'm going outside to play."

"Where were you? I think we missed our window of opportunity. He's outside," I say. My husband shrugs his shoulders and goes to make a pot of coffee preparing for a lengthy siege I guess.

Somebody has to do something. I go out on the back porch calling and calling using all the precious little names that I can think of for Dickens. But like a smart kid who knows what is in store for him, there is no Dickens. I know full well, however, that he is hiding somewhere in the bushes ready for a speedy retreat if I even try coming close to ambush him.

"Now we've blown it," I tell my husband in exasperation.

We consider our options. We know that it is too late to wish that we had done a better job getting Dickens under control when he was a kitten. I will be the one to hang my head and call the vet's office to reschedule if we don't get some results soon.

Just as I say this we hear the cat door swing open and in comes Dickens. We scramble into position. This time nobody yells or screams, and Dickens gets put in his crate. We load him into the car pretending not to hear his cries of disgust for us tricking him, and we leave the driveway in a rush of squealing tires.

What an ordeal! Sitting in the waiting room neither of us say anything to each other while our hearts beat loudly.

"Calm down. We've done it one more time," says my husband.

We look at all the other docile cats lounging regally in their crates making no big deal of being there. What must they think of this unruly and pampered boy?

It's too embarrassing to make much of our behavior when talking with the vet. We attempt to look cool and collected, but I suspect that he has seen enough frazzled owners in his career to know that we are well meaning, but amateurish in our pet control.

Oh, well. We don't have to worry about this until next year, or yikes— we have to kennel him while we go away in a couple weeks! Stay tuned to see if we can ever get it right.

An Adventure Unfolds in the Middle East

Over our traveling years, my husband and I have had more than the usual number of people jokingly wanting to be taken along tucked into our suitcase. On our recent trip we decided to honor one such request.

Stuffed into our luggage headed to Israel and Egypt was a little fellow named Flat Stanley. He made it through TSA security checks just fine. Evidently, he survived the mass of luggage stored in the cargo hold and tumbled down the baggage carousel all in one piece.

You see, a second grade great-nephew from Pennsylvania had sent us a letter a couple weeks prior to our trip asking if we would keep Flat Stanley, a paper cutout figure, for a short time. His class would like to hear from us about what adventures Flat Stanley would have around our area.

Little did our young nephew know that his Flat Stanley would travel away from New York, and perhaps go the furthest distance of any Flat Stanley sent from his classmates.

It only made sense that we take Flat Stanley with us neatly folded and placed carefully in a baggie for a smooth voyage. We wanted him to arrive at our destination wrinkle free just like our clothes. Our job, according to the instructions that came with him, was to take his picture near famous sights, write some pertinent information for second graders and provide a map of where Stanley visited.

"Flat Stanley," written by Jeff Brown and illustrated by Tomi Ungerer, has been around since 1964. It is the first in a series of books featuring Stanley Lambchop, a completely flat boy.

Stanley Lambchop is given a big bulletin board by his dad for displaying pictures and posters. Dad hangs it on the wall over Stanley's bed. During the night the board falls from the wall, flattening Stanley in his sleep. He survives and makes the best of his altered state, and soon he is entering locked rooms by sliding under the door, and playing with his younger brother as a kite. Stanley even helps catch art museum thieves by posing as a painting on the wall. But Stanley has one special advantage: he can now visit his friends by being mailed in an envelope.

Elementary teachers have embraced the Flat Stanley project for years. When my husband smoothed out Flat Stanley in the desert heat posing him for pictures near the pyramids and sphinx, all sorts of tourists yelled out greetings to Stanley proving what an international celebrity he has become.

It was when Flat Stanley came around children, though, that he really shined. We were fortunate to be invited to a home of a Cairo family for a meal and conversation one evening. Of course, Stanley went along in my husband's pocket waiting to engage with a new opportunity.

The family that greeted us was a multi-generational Muslim one. It wasn't long before friendly Aleyah, a fourth grader at a private international school, came over to talk with us. She spoke fluent English along with Arabic, German and French.

As soon as Flat Stanley came out of my husband's pocket, a big smile came over Aleyah's face.

"Do you know who he is?" my husband asked.

"I know all about Flat Stanley," she replied.

She wanted to hold Stanley and willingly posed for pictures. We learned more about her interests, and when we returned to our hotel room we jotted down some notes to share with the Pennsylvania classroom.

One morning we had the opportunity to visit a government school, an elementary school provided by tax dollars for all Egyptian children. Of course, Flat Stanley had to wiggle his way into all the photos with the giggling primary children.

There were two obvious differences from American schools: boys and girls were separated on two sides of the room, and their phonics was practiced in both in English and Arabic. The second graders sang "Twinkle, Twinkle Little Star" in English to entertain. Flat Stanley danced to the tune like he had heard it before.

In the meantime, with daily Flat Stanley pictures being sent via cell phone to our nephew, we discovered that he was so excited that he was writing his own Flat Stanley book.

When it was time to depart to the United States, we had to consider how we would carry Stanley back. By then he had become a special member of the trip. After some thought it was decided that Stanley would fly back in my husband's suitcase mummified. He was rolled up tightly and carefully placed into a small, decorated Egyptian sarcophagus for preservation.

Flat Stanley was returned to our nephew via the U.S. mail. The wee little guy was unrolled and told about his marvelous tag along adventure in the Middle East. We would love to have been in on that conversation!

Take Back Your Stuff

This is an open letter to all our grown children everywhere:

Come get your stuff that you have been storing in our basements, attics, sheds and spare bedrooms since—well, we've lost track of how long.

My husband and I were sorting and simplifying one summer feeling pretty good about ourselves when we came upon a maple bedroom set in the far corner of our shed.

"Do you suppose it's even missed?" asked my husband.

"I doubt it," I replied.

"Let's go ahead and put it up for sale. We'll give her [my daughter] the money. She's never going to use it again."

"I think that we need to ask her what she wants to do about it," I replied being the more diplomatic of the two in this case.

That evening we made a phone call, and got the most amazing answer in return.

"Why, I had no idea I still had that bedroom set."

My husband was nodding to me as if to say that he was right about it all along.

How could we have forgotten the scorching hot day moving the bedroom set in huffing and puffing the whole way? We shifted our possessions making room temporarily for a bulky headboard, dresser and bed rails. Were we in for a surprise that lasted ten years! At one point I had even thought about setting it up in the spare bedroom and using it. Would my daughter have noticed when she came visiting?

"What do you need the room for?" my daughter asked.— Then a bigger pause. "You're not moving, are you?"

Here's a grown child not getting it that her parents want the space for themselves to store their own stuff.

"We have lives, too," we reply in unison. I think that ended the conversation on that topic for another year or so.

Well, looking back I believe that I pulled the same stunt on my mother when I was younger. I was insensitive to her, and sadly her complaining fell on deaf ears. Every time I came to see her, eventually the conversation turned to when I was planning to get the last box or two filled with my old yearbooks and teenage memorabilia out of the tiny space in the attic. It was taking up room in a big house lived in by one occupant —for what, I couldn't figure out. Finally, after repeated warnings packages arrived on my doorstep. The message couldn't have been any clearer.

We have good friends that actually have had whole households of belongings stuffed into their place while their adult kids were moving from one job to another. We would be ushered around the boxes with a small wave of apology for the mess, and on to our visit. Those are pretty short-term inconveniences, though, and all parents try to do that for their kids. I wonder if all the stuff left when the big kids moved, though, or was some of it held back.

I am laughing to myself over my recently empty nesting friends who are claiming whole bedroom takeovers for offices and TV rooms with utter glee in their eyes. How long will they keep all the teenage vampire novels and girly posters on the walls before packing them away for safekeeping? That's how the whole vicious cycle begins I want to tell them. Next it will be college textbooks stored that might be needed for reference, but they've got four years to find room for them.

So what happened to the maple bedroom set? We sold it and sent a check off to our grown up kid. It was a win-win situation. She's never mentioned it again, because she knows that we have more boxes of her books stored, and we might be serious about our simplifying business.

Your Car's Interior Tells Your Story

I peeked inside a car window in the mall parking lot. It looked like someone had been on an "American Pickers" adventure of his own at a country auction or roadside sale.

From years of amateur sleuthing in preparation for writing my bestselling novel, I have discovered that there is no rhyme or reason to the make, model or condition of the car. From one price range to another, the interior can be an eye opener. Perish the thought though, that it could be the normal state of affairs.

Do you ever glance as you walk close to another car, or am I the only snoop that admits it? Sometimes it's the dog or two left behind that draws my eyes in. I can't help myself.

Which reminds me of someone who is a successful business executive that spends a major portion of her time commuting in her luxury car. Whatever her lame excuse (in my opinion), which I don't remember, the interior looked like a green trash receptacle on wheels. The employees of any McDonald's franchise are on their toes keeping the property pristine in contrast to her notion of sanitation.

She told me to shove things around to get comfortable. No kidding! In the meantime I was hoping my cloth coat wouldn't get destroyed with grease spots. The odor of stale coffee and breakfast sandwiches was pretty pungent, too. My shoes stayed in motion swatting wrappers away from my feet like mosquitoes at a campfire.

"Don't worry. I empty out my car every Saturday morning," she told me cheerfully.

"Why don't you throw out your trash after every visit through the drive-thru?"

"I don't have the time," she laughed. "What's the big deal?"

With the sticker price on her car, it should have come with a cleaning valet, too.

Well, it works for her lifestyle, and I should leave it at that.

Which reminds me of a musician who kept his entire file of sheet music back in the day on the rear seat of his Volkswagen bus like a floating performance center piled on high.

He was not a permanent fixture anywhere. He drifted from place to place without a care in the world. Why, all he had to do was reach over his shoulder, and his life was labeled in chronological order. He had invented his own cataloging system rivaling that of the New York City Public Library. Those cross country travels were his chance to write more lyrics and get in touch with his inner nature.

Which reminds me of being invited to sit in a kid proof van by a young parent. I am cushioned by car seats, assorted toys, DVDs and whatever else "live" is being transported—kids or not on board. As long as it's not too sticky, I can do fine in the short haul of matters. It's unfortunate that parents are so apologetic. Most of us have been there.

I went with my girlfriend and her daughter on a quick hour drive, and I laughed at the collection of artifacts the little one required in order to leave home. Half the town's library books were there for entertainment. Now there's nothing wrong with that, as reading is good all the time everywhere. Hopefully those due dates will be respected before too many get lost under the seat.

Which reminds me of a lady who shoved the dog blanket out of the front seat so I could sit down. Would it have been rude to pull out my handy clothes freshener spray first? I had on my best black pants. Was I being picky, or what? After all, she was doing the long trip driving graciously. I didn't have a thing to worry about, except that I'd forgotten to pack a lint brush in my suitcase.

Which reminds me of the time my husband had been in an auto accident. Several days later he couldn't move those sore body parts of his sufficiently to clean out his personal effects. The total wreck was parked waiting to be towed away to car heaven.

Besides, the car was so crunched up that only a small person would fit. I crawled in and inched around locating all sorts of articles down to candy wrappers and pennies under the floor mats. I left those. Even sitting there I was missing obvious items right in front of my nose like the CD still in the player, which never did come out. The whole time I was going through the car I was overwhelmed at the damage. If there had been a passenger, the ending would not have been so fortunate.

Which reminds me of people who literally have to live in their cars out of necessity, and here is where I come to the end of my playfulness. They are not so lucky, and I hope better for them soon.

There is no more inspiring story than that of Hilary Swank, a favorite actor of mine. As a teen with her recently divorced mother, they lived in the car until her mom could afford an apartment near LA. The rest is Hollywood.

When you see me out and about wandering through a parking lot, it might be that I have lost track of my car. Then again, it might not.

Did you really need to know all that?

I Seriously Wonder What Some People Think

Our modern world must have a problem of some sort out in the forefront, or folks are uncomfortable. This one is as good as any, and more entertaining than most. Perhaps, it brings out the extreme in attitude when there is so little wiggle room for personal freedom anymore.

I get a belly laugh noticing someone in the dead of winter wearing flip flops bundled up in a North Face parka jumping over a snow mound to get to the sidewalk. There is a shivering chatter to her toothy grin. My first reaction is to say, "yes, it is cold outside and haven't you noticed recently?" I butt out and watch the ascent thinking that this person has got to be on the college ski team to be that accurate with her footing. I'm jealous a bit. Sliding down a snowdrift landing on my derrière is not entertainment that I can chance anymore.

Go ahead and consider me off my rocker. I am a people watcher to the thirteenth degree, and the more bizarre scene in my estimation, the better. Certainly, I am not ridiculing or condemning at all. It's curiosity plain and simple, and I go along for the free ride.

A youthful tattoo with a boyfriend's name covering her shoulder blade sends a message to everyone else that this guy is claimed. Will it turn into an adult embarrassment when the guy is no longer in her life? I've heard too many stories of the likes. Even though tattoo art is appealing in its designs, I try to imagine how she will explain it to her children years later. Tattoo removal is possible, and might prove to be the best answer when the commitment is over permanently.

I take a second look when I see a little kid in the mall wearing her brand new Ugg boots with a halter-top in the heat of a sweltering summer day. They must be recently purchased and she can't wait for school to prance around with them for the world to see her. There is fashion sense to the outfit, and obviously she has noticed more than a few TV starlets doing the identical thing. It doesn't bother her that her other companions are in regular attire either. And she is her own person. I like that in her spunky self. I'll give her that in her favor. Other than that, her body must be burning up in sweat tramping along.

What's crazier than to see a guy suited up on fashionable Fifth Avenue lugging an expensive designer briefcase wearing a furry bomber hat pulled down over his ears to complement his business attire? Where is he going? To an audition? To a photo shoot? Anything goes in New York City and I guess I have seen just about everything there through the years. What a mecca for the latest fashion statement and room left over for the occasional 60s hippie.

I can't imagine taking a tour through the cobbled streets of Venice without sturdy walking shoes, but the local Italian women adorn the highest of stilettos and get away with it day in and day out. What infuriates me is these females look sleek from head to foot, too, not to mention sexy.

How I wished that I didn't appear like a rumpled tourist in my travel clothes identical to every other American on the road. My sensible L.L.Bean purse—not an exquisite leather one worth more than my monthly car payment, and my cheap sunglasses conceal my inner thoughts.

I look twice when I see a teenager in Wal-Mart schlepping along in oversized fuzzy, wuzzy bunny slippers. Apparently from the bedroom in the lounging fleece to the store aisles is all in a night's way to make shopping a form of entertainment. I am not going to let myself think what I would say if I were her mother. That's not my business. Of course, what I am doing out at that hour of the night is another thing.

What makes me chuckle is looking at a miniature dog dressed to the nines complete with bows in her hair in someone's arms. My eyes go back and forth between owner and pup before I make the connection that they look just alike. When I overhear the conversation and can't picture where the "second person" is, I realize that these two gals are out on the town woofing it up together. Here's hoping that they have a paw-fully good time.

I could go on and on. Hairstyles, make up and body piercings are worthy of examining. I think that I have made my point. Now it's your turn to take notice of what strikes your fancy. Don't take it all too seriously either.

Still Waiting for Your E-Mail

"Better late than never," is a line of defense that individuals have exploited for decades. Hearing those words ruffle my feathers, however. They fall a hair short of the classic, "the dog ate my homework."

There is a new theory that I believe has tipped the balance in the opposite direction. The expression is an old cliché. For better or worse, it has taken on new meaning in our technological world.

"No news is good news."

My take is that people don't reply electronically.

Naturally, I had to check out what Emily Post said about answering correspondence. She's always been my "go-to" reference in matters of social grace.

All I had to do was Google, and voila, there was Post's ten ways for proper etiquette in e-mail correspondence. The topic turns out to be the first of many entries on the page concerning new 21st century behavior.

Several of Post's comments are such common sense that I can't imagine why she has to spell them out. Children learn the rules of basic etiquette, and later as adults they recognize its potential value in maintaining interpersonal connections. The rub comes more than likely in putting the rules faithfully into practice. Laziness, you say?

Evidently not answering e-mails is tolerated in the work world. Will it become the norm—or has it already, and I am behind the eight ball?

I had to ask. Financial planners, teachers, coaches and real estate agents responded. More than one career person told me the honest truth. I walked away dumbfounded. It was what I suspected all along.

A salesman said that it used to be that he could never get a straight answer out of a client without committing to a lot of face-to-face time. It took skill and persistence. Today, he claims that it is far worse. He gets no answers whatsoever from e-mailing. It's the great elusive indecisiveness that bothers him the most. People don't like to commit to any decision.

Another man replied that he never gets his manager to give his OK. He does a lot more on assumption than previously. He stresses that he is a self-directed employee, and that is a win-win for both. However, he said he nervously waits for the other shoe to fall from the corporation twenty-four hours a day.

Emily Post says to respond always, even if it is a brief note.

I'll accept the one or two word e-mails from my colleagues. Short and sweet save a load of time. There's no problem there. I figure that it is better to get a brief message than never hear back from someone. Besides, that falls into the category of general good manners.

Yes. Yes. Emily Post says that in professional e-mailing your image and reputation is at stake. She firmly recommends that you watch your spelling and grammar. In addition, you should look over what you write before you press, "send." And save the "cutesy" comments for personal e-mailing. It has no place in the office.

Another thing that Post emphasizes is not mixing professional and personal into the same e-mail.

My boss doesn't care that my beloved dog was put to sleep at the vet's office and I am inconsolable. He reads my incoherent message saying that I will be several days late meeting a deadline.

Nor does my employer give a hoot that right now I am watching the waves roll in on Laguna Beach— only dreaming, and there is spotty Wi-Fi. He wants my full work attention, and that is fair enough. I'll head back to surfing the Internet in the hotel lobby.

The terrific thing for those who operate out of a home office is that you can disregard office dress code. It doesn't mean failing to keep on top of e-mail correspondence, even if you are clever enough to avoid Skyping in your "jammies" before 9 a.m.

There's something else at stake that has to do with how one handles "messaging." It all boils down to the age group you are communicating with it, and it doesn't take a rocket scientist to figure it out either.

Granted all my brief interviews were with folks well entrenched in the workforce. There is something else in play for younger people that change the perspective a trifle.

My teenage neighbor tells me that texting is the way she makes plans with her friends and keeps track of her part-time waitress shift schedule. She never uses e-mailing anymore. If I want to hear from her, she politely informs me then I need to text. She resists answering her cell phone, too.

Rather than complain, I learn a colleague's patterns quickly and accept how he communicates— might it be phone, texting, e-mailing.

Again, simply learning to maneuver around someone's habits makes you less frustrated. I didn't find anything from Post on that one.

On her website, Emily Post stresses that business etiquette is a vital piece of the professional success puzzle. From job interviewing to hosting business meals, from making the phone call to landing the deal, etiquette, image and the ability to convey your "brand" are what make the lasting impression is all about.

There are far too many situations and types of personalities that you must manage to allow carelessness, rudeness, or whatever you want to label it, to interfere. You can count on me. I will be answering your e-mail in a jiffy.

The Best Christmas Present Ever

In our household we abandoned the craziness of the holiday season a decade ago, and it was the best present that we ever gave each other. The unadorned pleasure of the season makes up for it tenfold!

Last week I sat down with former colleagues for our annual holiday get together, and instead of exchanging gifts, we contributed to the local food pantry.

Likewise, with a group of multi-generational women friends we shared favorite memories of Christmas. A few of those recollections were from decades ago. Love and laughter were our gifts to each other. I'll still be chuckling over those stories way into the winter months!

Today the world is so conscious of being politically correct that yes, I momentarily hesitated before writing these memories. However, I offer them to you for what they are worth respectful of folks having different beliefs than mine.

Years ago I knew that I had found the man of my dreams when my future husband handed me a fruitcake as an early gift.

How many couples do you know who both actually crave a well made fruitcake, and for a hobby spend hours hunting for the perfect one? We have ordered from companies all over the map, and shopped in the most unusual places searching for the ever elusive delicacy.

During one of my earliest teaching years when I was pretty naïve, I gave out the best Christmas present ever without realizing it.

Our classroom was decorated with a lovely real tree with lights that shimmered magically all day long. I had the false assumption that all my students were living in situations where they were anticipating the same Christmas trimmings.

"What are you going to do with the tree when school is out over vacation," asked a gangly boy who always seemed to be curious about things.

"Why, I don't know," I replied believing that the custodian would take it away and put it on the dump pile at the back of the building.

I didn't think anymore about it, and totally missed the cue from the boy.

Two days later he came and asked the same question. Thank goodness he was persistent!

This time I wised up and realized that he might want that tree. I asked him outright.

"Oh, thank you. My brother and I will take it home, but can we wait until all the others are gone so no one will know?"

My heart immediately went out to him and we made a plan that the tree would be his with no questions asked.

The day arrived when the two brothers hauled off the tree, and watching from the classroom window I had tears in my eyes as they slowly plodded through the street dragging the tree behind them.

"You don't have a tree for the rubbish pile?" asked the custodian standing in my doorway right then surveying the room.

"No tree."

The custodian walked off accepting that short reply. If he had seen the boy and his brother carrying the tree down the stairwell leaving its needles behind, he never mentioned it again.

The last Christmas that I ever spent time with my father at home was a most challenging one because of nasty weather issues in Rochester.

By the time the delayed plane landed on Long Island it was way late into the afternoon, and my parents had left the relatives behind at the Christmas turkey dinner to pick me up.

I put my dad's hand in mine and helped him walk to the parking lot, and I sensed that this was a sacred moment between him and me. Who cared if we had leftovers when we got home? It was the loving moment that I recall every Christmas season.

Having never lived in the country, the first year of our marriage I wanted to cut down our very own Christmas tree. My new husband took me to a friend's land up on the hill. He was less enthusiastic than me having always been a country boy, yet he went along with the plan playing up to my excitement.

"You chop down the tree and I will take photos," my husband said putting all the required tools into the trunk of the car.

Off we hiked in a blinding snowstorm up the hill until I spotted the perfect tree. I set to work and sawed and sawed, but it didn't seem like I was even making a dent in the bark. I took off my jacket and kept at it, but I realized then that this was not going to be easy at all.

"You're doing this all wrong. You are making too much work of it. Work smarter," my husband said.

After a few more attempts, I gave up and my husband finished the job. By the time we hauled the tree down to the house, our friends had warm coffee waiting. They also broke the news to us that we had strayed way off their land and had chopped down a neighbor's tree.

The second bad news came when we got the tree home, and even with a cathedral ceiling in our living room, the tree wouldn't fit unless it was bent in two. I guess things looked smaller out in nature!

My gift to you: tuck your precious memories away in your heart forever. No finer gift will you receive.

A Variety Pack of Friendships Suits Me Well

I've lost count of the types of friendships that make up my life.

All I know is that they function together like cogs in a wheel to make me the person that I am.

Work friends. Family friends. Virtual friends. Childhood friends. It doesn't matter at what stage I am in, there is someone out there willing to engage in friendship with me if I take notice.

Don't get me wrong. I am not a collector of friends in the sense of them being objects rattling around in my life waiting for the right usefulness.

"True happiness consists not in the multitude of friends, but in their worth and choice," said Samuel Johnson, eighteenth century British writer.

Through social media sites, such as Facebook, I have a group of friends that I share with that I rarely if ever socialize with in real time. In fact, when we do pass at some function, or on the street, we just smile in recognition leaving it at that. Yet we often express our deepest concerns and relate to the joys in daily life together. We electronically hug each other over college degrees, loss of family members and new babies. We trade reviews of fine places to eat, and unique bed and breakfast establishments worthy of notice. We enjoy each other's pictures and travels.

Stieg Larsson's character Mikael Blomkvist in "The Girl with the Dragon Tatoo" said, "Friendship-my definition—is built on two things. Respect and trust. Both elements have to be there. And it has to be mutual. You can have respect for someone, but if you don't have trust, the friendship will crumble."

Once a friendship is set into motion, whatever the reason, it follows Newton's Law of Physics about momentum. Old Newton was a wise man for sure. Certainly, there are those relationships with other people for reasons of drastic change in values and lifestyle make it impossible to continue together. You drift apart and perhaps it is for the best. Once in awhile you might check to see if you can continue on together. Somehow in the beginning you found enough mutual interests that drew you together.

For a long time I taught in a very close knit community of teachers. We went through marriages, babies, divorces and deaths of family members within the brick walls. It only bonded us closer as people. Now as retirees we meet faithfully for monthly lunches continuing sharing together. As we age we are finding that we are supporting each other emotionally going through illnesses and surgeries; we are encouragement to those who are intensive caregivers for husbands. I had that network when I was younger. Why shouldn't it continue?

What a surprise when I am making a new business acquaintance and we end up discovering that our lives parallel! Outside the business realm we become good friends. At least, we have not limited ourselves and not let the relationship bud. More often than not, I come back from an interview enthusiastic because I have met a person with similar interests.

Then the other constant in a friendship is that less time spent together doesn't necessarily imply a lukewarm relationship. Ouch! That is particularly hard for some personalities that demand a lot from a friendship. It is a matter of sharing every little thing. And I don't think that it is only women either. The intriguing thing about a strong relationship is that the occasional phone call or visit will put you right back into each other's lives like there was no gap whatsoever. The conversation continues on and on.

True, it's your women friends that do the marathon shopping with you—not all of them, though. Others are your book club friends and your gym friends.

I appreciate the friend that will listen to me, especially when there is a major problem. I need undivided attention. I need a hug and some empathy. I don't want to listen to their problems right then. That diminishes mine to relative second place on the scale.

Loyalty counts in my opinion. "If a man does not make new acquaintance as he advances through life, he will soon find himself left alone. A man should keep his friendship in constant repair," said Samuel Johnson.

At the end of each year when I am looking back on it, I think of all the new friends who have showed up in my life all because of the exits that I have taken on the road. Sometimes I am surprised. Other times I am overwhelmed that a person has reached out in friendship that I wouldn't have expected. Occasionally an old friendship blooms again thanks to one or the other of us taking the initiative.

It makes me smile. What a wonderful way to start a new year, too, without those pesky resolutions hanging over my head. Instead, I will focus on friends and live the next twelve months well.

.

Four Things I Have No Doubt About

The glass half full or half empty notion spills into the everyday flow of life.

You might assume that carrying around a married name like mine cast me in the doubters' category by default. Naturally, it has made for a lot of joking comments throughout the years.

I haven't succumbed to its tugging and let it overtake my outlook. I keep my optimistic nature, no doubt about it.

You must know a "doubting Thomas" or two. They can be hard to take in large doses, wouldn't you say? Often they become the "back burner" friends that you turn on occasionally. The rest of the time you let them simmer and season.

When that questioning attitude is used for good, remarkable things have happened in history. Many a skeptic envisioned the best inventions—Fulton's steamship better known as Fulton's Folly, Edison's telephone and Henry Ford's automobile. You can't forget Steve Jobs either!

However, like any other person living on the planet there are things that I seriously doubt.

No. 1— I seriously doubt that potholes will disappear off the radar and out of my path any time in the foreseeable future.

It's like my car is a magnet and drawn to every possible one for a few seconds with its teeth jarring pain. I am suspended in mid- air waiting for one of my four tires to hit the ground. Thunk!

I am in the wrong expressway lane at precisely the wrong time. I could be on the wrong country road and there's lots of room to maneuver. It doesn't matter. Potholes find me and sink me.

To make matters worse, I actually walked right into one yesterday when I was on foot. Do you doubt that?

The weather was gorgeous and everyone in the neighborhood was out taking stock of the land. The neighbor girls called out to me. I wasn't paying attention to where I was heading. Lucky me. I didn't twist my ankle.

No. 2—I seriously doubt that we have heard the last of Marilyn Monroe.

Just when there is a lull, another movie, television series or book on Marilyn surfaces. Someone writes a biography revealing that he spent one week with her during a movie shoot, and now we have a fresh slice through the curtain of mystery.

Apparently, there is still money to be made, and you can't beat capitalizing on someone even when she is long gone and can't speak back. After all, there is a new generation or two to entice.

Don't misinterpret me here. Marilyn was an amazing icon, and her disappearance off the horizon was tragic. I watched her movies and read the "real truth" and the half-truth depending upon the particular author's motive.

She deserves her glory, but enough is enough. Has Hollywood learned any lessons from Marilyn's life, or does fame continue to rock a few stars failing to cope with addictions?

No. 3— Traveling the "friendly" skies will not get any more congenial in the near future.

Civility has been thrown out the window even if I am luck to get the seat closest to the view. People are rude, messy and invasive of my armrest.

The aisle seat isn't much better with its purported freedom to get up and move in the cabin. One or other of my seatmates constantly must crawl over me and step on my toes like I am bread dough waiting to be punched.

If I can hold out until I am 75, I won't get the full body scan. And I won't have to bend down to untie my shoes and struggle to get them back on while the young kid behind me pushes me out of the way onward and upward.

In the meantime, I am surprised when my flight arrives on time and it is best to leave it at that.

No. 4— I doubt being put on hold on the phone will get any shorter.

I've learned to multi-task the time to the point of forgetting what the call was about in the first place. Well, I might be exaggerating, but you get my drift.

When I do get the occasional sincere customer service person, I rejoice and forget all about the wait time. It's not worth the worry.

The other day the automated voice asked me if I wanted music or not during my wait. How considerate! Which number could I press to get my coffee served?

Whew! All that's off my chest. Now I can get on to getting rid of mosquitoes, escalating gas prices, people talking in the movies and political phone surveys.

You seriously doubt that, you say?

ACKNOWLEDGMENTS

The greatest piece of writing advice that I ever received came from an unknown source: make your point with a punch and move on. I have tried to do that and leave the wordiness to others.

I am grateful for meticulous editing by DJ Smith, someone I have depended on regularly to pick apart my manuscripts. He possesses an uncanny sixth sense in knowing the appropriate time to step in with constructive advice; he understands when not to tamper too much with an essay allowing my voice to speak through loud and clear.

Mark Gillespie had faith in my writing abilities, and stood back to watch them take form in an opinion column that has become popular with readers. His kind words in the Foreword make me appreciate his love of the written word.

I am appreciative of the readers of my column, blog and Facebook page. They continually remind me why I need to share my stories, although at one time I would have been considered a shy child.

Finally, there has to be one person who gets the brunt of hearing essays and columns over and over when they are in the beginning stages. It can be painful to say the least to live with a writer. Everything must be pushed aside, including conversations, to get down the thoughts for the latest deadline. I am no better or worse than any other author. Thanks, Larry. I hope that my pieces have been enlightening to you, too. Your stunning cover and graphics capture visually what's needed to compliment the words.